The Purpose of You

Discover the Best You
Your Future Deserves Your Attention!

Fiona Inc.
www.fionainc.com

Published, First Edition April 2012, Second Edition September 2012
Fiona Inc.
www.fionainc.com
717-917-8101

Unless otherwise identified, Bible quotations in this book are from the Amplified and the King James versions of the Bible.

Special Thanks To

My husband who has been a very BIG help during the writing of this book and our many years of marriage.

My wonderful sons Gabriel and Josiah, you are my cheerleaders.

My parents, the Surujpauls, for the awesome life example that you show me.

My mother and father-in law, the Pyszkas, for being a great family support.

My friends and family who have been diligent in helping with the writing of this book and the support of my purpose.

Most of all to my Lord and Savior Jesus, my Heavenly Father, God, and my greatest teacher, The Holy Spirit.

Thank You. I am most grateful!

Introduction

It seems the question today that everyone is searching for the answer to is, "who am I?" With this is paired the equally curious question of "What am I doing here?" These unanswered questions have sent many to an early grave in most cases self-inflicted and unfulfilled. It's a question of identity and purpose.

It is estimated that over 21 million American children and adults deal with depression annually. The report further states that it is the leading cause for disability in Americans ages 15 to 44. *("© copyright Mental Health America" April 16, 2012.)*

Now if you or someone you know has ever suffered from depression, then you know these statistics to be not just numbers, but reality.

Depression, in my opinion, stems from not being able to be who you would really like to be, around the people you would like to spend your time with. Of course that's just my opinion, which I would like to ask you to consider for just a moment as you read the rest of this book.

Though this book is not about depression, it is about purpose and identity. Your identity can be hidden or stolen during bouts of depression, lack of knowledge or merely being in a controlling environment. Your purpose is lost if your identity stays unknown.

Over the years I have met with many people who have been aggravated at life because of some reason or the other. The root cause has always boiled down to unmet expectations by others.

Whether someone mistreated you or you expected them to know more than they do, it was a disappointment. These disappointments can lead you to a life of compromise or conflict. You live with bottled up expectations not being expressed, or maybe expressed to the wrong group of people. You know, the friends you talk to on the phone to share your disappointments about people. These conversations can lead to gossip and other ungodly behaviors that start a cycle of negativity.

Negativity is a fruit of unfulfilled purpose. Negativity can cause the brightest idea to be smashed into pieces. It leaves shattered shreds all around, piercing the footsteps of those who step into its wandering particles.

This book brings good news that will give you the right perspective about who you were created to be, what you should do about it, and how you can keep your identity from being stolen, lost or merely kept in the dark. This book will help you discover the best about you.

Today is your day. You are on your way up to a whole new level of living. Your days of the unknown are over. Your life of fullness must go on. You were created with a unique identity for a marvelous purpose, by our amazing heavenly Father.

So come along with me for this incredible journey to explore your identity and find your purpose, what it means and how you can claim it back, clean it up or put it to work for you.

No matter your level of spirituality, physical maturity or education, you can benefit from the cutting edge, insightful message of this book.

It's not who you are, but who you were meant to be! Your future deserves your attention.

Fiona Pyszka

Contents

Foreword

Who am I? Why was I born? What am I doing here? All questions that the average person has asked themselves one time or other in their lives. Against the backdrop of an ever expanding universe or even a world that is so diverse and complicated that it boggles the imagination, it seems as though our purpose for being born shrinks in comparison. Yet, according to the Word of God, the Bible, each one of us was born through divine design and each of us was born to fulfill a specific purpose orchestrated by God Himself.

The search for self-worth and self-significance can be an exercise in futility, consuming a lifetime of endless pursuit and self-examination, unless one knows where to start in their search and how to walk that, at times, volatile road of introspection and reflection. Fiona Pyszka has shown us all where to start our journey and how to proceed step by step in her new book, *The Purpose of You*. Beginning with an assumption of truth that all who are born are precious in God's sight and are worthy of life, she challenges us to take God at His word and accept the *fact* that each of us are special, with a specific purpose and are significant enough to Him that He gave His only Son, Jesus, as a sacrifice to ensure that we would live with Him forever. She then teaches us how to identify deceptions and pit-falls placed in our path by our enemy in an attempt to side track our walk in God's significance for us, and how to identify the instructions of God, through His Word, that successfully counterbalances these deceptions and keeps us on the path of God's significance, laid out for us by God Himself.

If you have struggled with self-significance, unworthiness, a lack of self-confidence, questions concerning "why me," or "who am I;" have faced the personal emotional monsters of no confidence, insecurity. Or have been victimized by emotional, spiritual or physical trauma or abuse that has resulted in you developing a personality characteristic of worthlessness, triviality, insignificance, and bitterness or hatred of self, then this book, *The Purpose of You,* is the one resource that is a must for you.

Dr. Ron Charles,
Missionary to Egypt and author of "The Search"

Chapter One

What's in a Name?

"Your name is the first introduction of who you are to every person you meet in your lifetime."- **Fiona Pyszka**

A good name is more desirable than great riches; to be esteemed is better than silver or gold. **Proverbs 22:1**

What's in a name? Did you know that everyone will say their name hundreds of times in their lifetime? Of those times, it would have been used as a first-time introduction. Yet many people would admit that they don't like their name, or their name reminds them of someone they are working hard to "not be like".

Our name is so important to our purpose and future that in some cases God changed the names of people that He ordained to do certain things for Him. He personally named the first human, Adam. Then Adam named Eve. When those names were given, the reason for the name was given as well. In Genesis 3:20, Adam names his wife in the middle of the story of the fall of man. Adam gave her a name of life, when death was the consequence of their sin.

In Song of Solomon 1:3, we see the expression of how Solomon's name sounds to the listener,

> *Song of Solomon 1:3 3[And she continues] The odor of your ointments is fragrant; your name is like perfume poured out. Therefore do the maidens love you.*

". . . your name is like perfume poured out." Wow, what a compliment! We find out that his name is a pleasant smell that leaves an aroma of comfort and security. Jesus is such a name. His name is above all names, everywhere. Whether in heaven or earth, we can find no higher name.

> *Philippians 2:9 [9]Therefore [because He stooped so low] God has highly exalted Him and has freely bestowed on Him the name that is above every name,*

If the emphasis of the power of Jesus is placed so highly on His name, what does it mean to us when it comes to our name? In Proverbs 22:1, Solomon emphasizes a good name being more desirable than silver or gold, the currency used at that time.

> *Proverbs 22:1 A GOOD name is rather to be chosen than great riches, and loving favor rather than silver and gold.*

Let's put it in perspective. Would you be interested in doing business with a rich person who had the reputation for being corrupt and unreasonable? I would venture to say not. The same concept applies, would you do business with a wise, honorable, stable person, who might not be as rich? Absolutely yes should be the answer of a wise person!

Even so, your name is worth your attention today. For today's assignment I would like you to consider evaluating the value you put on your name and the reasons for them. Put some thought into why you feel the way you do, why you respond the way you do, and why you like or dislike when people call you by a certain name. Maybe you're someone whose name is John and people have been calling you Johnny since you were a little boy, so now you're stuck with it. You might not like it because it reminds you of "little Johnny". Or you might love your name because when you hear Johnny it reminds you of being favored or fun to be around. No matter the reason, take time now to resolve how you view your name. For the rest of this exercise I will use the phrase "your name" in reference to speaking of you.

Purpose Break

1. What is your name? _____

2. Do you like your name?_____

3. Why or why not? *(be thorough, for example: I don't like my last name because it's my divorced name, or I like my first name because my dad named me).* Then, write about how you feel when you hear your name or say your name. _____

_____

_____

_____

_____

_____

Evaluate

As you review how your name makes you feel, evaluate your experience with how people have responded to your name. For example, when they hear that "Mary" is coming do they run and hide, shout for joy, or could care less? At first, as you do this exercise, you might think it is frivolous or even a bit ridiculous. However, if you look at the emphasis that God placed on names, it might change your mind. So ask yourself these further questions:

How does your name affect people? Does it bring freedom or fear?

Let's look at an example: In Acts 9 we see Saul (later called Paul in Acts 13). Saul was the name that Christians feared, so his name affected them negatively. However, his name was changed to be a highlight of the New Testament. It seems his name was changed at the time that the men were instructed to separate Paul and Barnabas (see Acts 13) to go fulfill their unique purpose. From that time on in the Bible, we see that Saul was now called Paul (see Acts 13:9).

4. Do you believe you can change a negative feeling or reputation of your name?_____

5. Do you think it's necessary? _____

Jesus had negative connotations to His name (see Matthew 9:3-7). He was constantly questioned by His opposition. Jesus knew where His identity came from. It came from His Father (see Matthew 16:17; John 5:19).

What if you can't change your name? Look at 1 Chronicles 4:9-11.It tells the story of Jabez. A few verses in the Bible that show how God is interested in His people being God's best and not living with the labels people give us. Now consider this, do you think God can make you larger than your name says?

Decision

Today you have to make the decision that you will be obedient to God's will for your life. This includes how God wants to use your name on the earth. We see how God established the name of these people in the Bible:

1. Jeremiah 32:19-21 – How God made a name for His people.

2. Genesis 17:5 – God changed Abram's name to Abraham – one letter "h" added a multiplication factor to his name. He went from being "high ex-alted father" (Abram), to a "father of multitudes" (Abraham).

3. Genesis 17:15 - We see the same one letter change in Sarai's name to Sarah, Abraham's wife. God upgraded her name as well. You see God's plan for his chosen people was hinged on Sarah giving birth to a son by Abraham.

Make these decisions today

1. How will you see yourself from this day forth? _

_____

_____

_____

_____

2. When you introduce yourself or you hear your name, will there be added confidence and purpose behind how you speak about yourself? ___

_____

_____

_____

_____

_____

_____

3. List a few good qualities about you that you would like everyone to associate with your name? _____

_____

_____

_____

Your Future

Based upon your decision to make changes today, in the next year, do you anticipate that the value of your name will increase? _____

Chapter Two
Who Do You Say You Are?

"Your words about yourself determine the response you receive from your enemies and your friends."- Fiona Pyszka

And he saith unto them, But whom say ye that I am? And Peter answereth and saith unto him, Thou art the Christ. - Mark 8:29

Recently I was on the telephone with some vendors looking for the best fit for our family need. The list I started with was a result of recommendations by people who have used their services before. A few were from my own experiences. Either way, it was the good testimony and experience that caused me to even consider calling them. Because I had the benefit of recommendations it made looking for new services easier. In the same way, a good recommendation of you will cause people to consider you even if they've never heard of you. I ended up calling some of the vendors because of the good results I saw already from the people who have used them.

A business interested in growth would never print bad reviews of themselves. Their brochures that con-

9

tain all of their products and services will never even hint at any inadequacies they possess. Instead, they spotlight their most celebrated qualities. They highlight testimonials of raving customers, they list the names of "high profile" clients that they've worked with. All of this information allows a new customer to see the credibility the company holds. It gives evidence as to why people would want to associate and do business with them.

Yet when it comes to our individual lives, we tend to do the opposite. You find that people start sharing their inadequacies early in a relationship so as to not be "too good to be true". This type of thinking stems from a self image that indicates you don't want to think more highly of yourself than you ought to. Yet, if you look closely you will realize that saying the great stuff that's really true about you is not thinking more highly of yourself, but in fact, thinking exactly in line with who you are. It's the images of yourself that you keep alive in your mind's eye that ends up being the trademark of what you're known for. How is that possible?

You will always speak words about yourself in line with how you think about yourself. I often say to a

10

group when I'm speaking: "You couldn't pay me one million dollars or hold a gun to my head to make me speak badly about myself". Why not? Because I expect the words I say to come to pass. If I live a life expecting the words I say to produce what I say, then I should realize that both the negative and positive words I speak will come to pass.

So what does it mean to speak badly about yourself? Have you ever heard someone say how clumsy they are or how they always have "bad luck"? Have you ever heard someone say: "Oh yeah, I'm always the one who gets sick in our family", or "I'm the one everybody takes advantage of." Here's another one you hear quite often, "I always attract the losers." Have you ever noticed that these things always are true for the lives of the people saying these words? How about you? Let's do your image checkup.

How do you speak about yourself? Do you think that if you say too much about yourself that you may appear as a know-it-all? If you have been approached by someone to help them solve a problem, the last thing they need to hear is all of your inadequacies. They would rather hear your expertise or your recommendation of someone that could help solve their problem. The reason they came to you is to ask for your help in solving their problem. That makes you a problem solver, not a know-it-all.

A problem solver solves problems. They don't point things out without a possible recommendation for a solution. A person who just points out a problem with no viable solutions for restoration or repair is simply a complainer. From such people stay FAR, FAR away.

> James 5:9 tells us, "Do not complain, brethren, against one another, so that you [yourselves] may not be judged. Look! The Judge is [already] standing at the very door."

It's one thing to point out that something is unacceptable or not up to standard; however, when someone is a complainer they give off a very poignant smell (bad attitude) and will cause people to want to run from them. Examine yourself for such behavior and make a decision now to withdraw from having that kind of attitude. You will see positive changes in your friendships, your business relationships and your personal relationships.

Check your friendship list and see the quality of people you hang out with. Look at the type of people you give access to speak into your life. If they are always speaking about the past hurts and pains they've gone through without it being an example of restoration or triumph, then you have locked friendship with the wrong type of ship. It's the "ship" that's going in a direction that leads to death not life.

Your friendships and mentors, the people who speak into and influence your life, should be people that agree with the positive future you are dreaming about yourself. They should have positive stories and wise words to help you along the way of fulfilling your dreams and destiny. If you start sharing your dreams with someone and they share how they've tried that and it didn't work, you might want to reconsider telling them anymore.

A group in the Bible that had a negative view of their image was the Israelites when they were in the wilderness. In Numbers 13 we see the story of twelve men who were sent in as spies. Ten came back with an evil report, while two were very adamant that they could take the land. However, the ten spies thought that they were grasshoppers in comparison to the inhabitants of their promise land, they even went as far as saying that the inhabitants also thought they were grasshoppers,

> *Numbers 13:33* [33]*There we saw the Nephilim [or giants], the sons of Anak, who come from the giants; and we were in our own sight as grasshoppers, and so we were in their sight.*

Do you see how their image of themselves was projected as an assumption of what they thought the inhabitants of the land thought of them? Take a moment to consider if you allow this in your life. Many people live or work in a negative environment that tells them what they can't do more than what they can do, these atmospheres can be overcome you're your words. Say your words about you louder than the words you hear around you. The loudest way to say your words is through your actions. Do what God tells you to do, not what the negative people around you insist you do.

Numbers 14:24 talks about Caleb having a different spirit. The Lord admired that different spirit in Caleb, and as a result rewarded him with the land he spied out for him and his descendents.

> *Numbers 14:24* [24]*But My servant Caleb, because he has a different spirit and has followed*

Me fully, I will bring into the land into which he went, and his descendants shall possess it.

Caleb's different spirit prevented him from dying with the other thousands of complainers that the 10 spies were able to convince were losers and could not inhabit the land God chose for them. The enemy wants you to see yourself as a loser. You must continue to express who you are in Christ (more on this in a later chapter).

Imagine that the group of twelve men made it into the land as spies. First of all, if you are spies, the inhabitants of the land should not be able to recognize you, you should be able to blend in and look just like you were one of them. However, 10 0f these men already had a "grasshopper" image of themselves, they took that with them on their "spy" assignment. Their image of themselves projected a false report that caused an entire generation to lose out on what God promised them they could have. Don't lose out on what God has for you because of someone or group that does not believe God's Will for your life to be real or true. It was God's will for the children of Israel to take the promise land.

Numbers 13 1And the Lord said to Moses, 2Send men to explore and scout out [for your-selves] the land of Canaan, which I give to the Israelites. From each tribe of their fathers you shall send a man, every one a leader or head among them.

Let's take a moment here and consider what might have happened in generations before you? How did your ancestors' language affect you today? What is your family known for? Whether good or bad, these are things to evaluate and think about. We will have an opportunity to do so at the end of the chapter. However, just take a moment and consider some of the traits or behaviors that you have been carrying on as a tradition for generations now, that are in direct opposition to where you should really be going.

The only way to stop doing something is to stop doing it. It is as simple as that. Stop doing what was being done and start doing something new. Our words are powerful and one place to start is with what we say and how we say things about ourselves. From this moment on, make a decision that you will only say of yourself what is true of who you should really be, not the "who" that you have become because of what the generations before you have dictated, or the circumstances around you have aggravated.

So what's the end of the story in Numbers 13? Forty years later, Joshua (one of the 12 spies that agreed with Caleb), led the new generation into the "promised land" that their parents never got to see. Caleb went to the land (a mountain) that he had spied out 40 years earlier and told the giants to get off his land (see Joshua 15). These were the only two households that entered the "promise land" with someone from the generation God made the promise to.

When Joshua sent in the two spies to spy out the land before his invasion, they went to Rahab's house and she told them how much the people were terrified of them when they heard of all the miracles God had done for them

> Joshua 2:9-119And she said to the men, I know that the Lord has given you the land and that your terror is fallen upon us and that all the in- habitants of the land faint because of you. 10For we have heard how the Lord dried up the water of the Red Sea for you when you came out of Egypt, and what you did to the two kings

of the Amorites who were on the [east] side of the Jordan, Sihon and Og, whom you utterly destroyed. 11When we heard it, our hearts melted, neither did spirit or courage remain any more in any man because of you, for the Lord your God, He is God in heaven above and on earth beneath.

The miracles she was referring to were the Red Sea parting and the provision and all the things God had done for them 40 years earlier. You see, the enemy of Israel forty years earlier was more scared of Israel than Israel knew. However, because of their poor "grasshopper" self-image, they thought their enemy saw them as they saw themselves. Therefore, they defeated themselves with their own words.

Let's take a moment and examine your own self-image and the words that you speak about yourself and what you think people say about you.

Purpose Break

1. Describe the first "good" words that come to mind when you think of yourself. For example, if you were asked to introduce yourself to an audience, what would you say about yourself:

_____

_____

_____

_____

_____

_____

_____

_____

_____

_____

2. Do you believe those words and would you actually use them in a "live" introduction, or are
   these words what you would love to hear said
   about you, but are not convinced that you are
   these things? Why?

_____

_____

_____

_____

_____

_____

3. What words do you actually use to describe
   yourself now? (Think of when you speak of

yourself to friends and family.) :

_____

_____

_____

_____

4. Do you want to live the rest of your life the ac-
    cording to the negative words of your past or
    would you like to rewrite your future to include
    words that say who you would really like to be?
    If yes, then what are some of the words you
    would like to use to describe your "ideal" fu-
    ture?

_____

_____

_____

_____

_____

_____

_____

5. What do you see yourself doing in the future,
    that you've hidden or thought you weren't good
    enough to do? Do you want to start a busi-

ness? Teach a class? Go back to school?

_____

_____

_____

_____

_____

_____

_____

Evaluate

As you dream again of your future, the one that you really would like to see happen, keep in mind it should contain instructions that God has given you. Things that you know your family should have probably been doing but no one was able to ever seem to get it together to do. Maybe you're the one that can resurrect that dream again. Abraham was told to go where his father did not go. His father had the first instruction to go, but didn't. He stopped half way. Then, God told Abraham to leave his father and country and go to a place that He would show him (see Genesis 12).

List the obstacles that you know or think exist. Then next to them I want you to mark that you are able to take this land. Go ahead you can do it.

21

_____

_____

_____

_____

_____

Decision

Decide that you will stop agreeing with people's bad evaluation of you. This may take a few tries to get people used to the new you. However, if you don't enforce it, it won't yield the results of the best you.

Make these decisions today

1. Write a statement that would describe yourself (if you were a business) that would cause customers to want to choose your business (the new you) over your competitor (the old you) __

   _____

   _____

   _____

   _____

   _____

   _____

   _____

2. List the new words you want to say about yourself each day. A good practice would be to say them in the morning while you get dressed, in the car while you're traveling or anytime you can fit it in. The goal is to have repetition. It seems strange, but this is all about getting the best out of you. You have to *say* the best about you to *have* the best about you actually become reality _____

_____

_____

Chapter Three
You Don't Have to Fail to Succeed?

"Failure is not the required path for a successful life."-
Fiona Pyszka
*"Love never fails..." - **1 Corinthians 13:8***

I remember when I was a little girl asking my dad one night as we drove down the highway, "How do you keep from not running into the oncoming traffic when their lights are so bright as they come towards you". I will never forget his response. He told me, "Keep your focus on your side of the road. If you look on their side at their lights, you will automatically start heading towards them." What great advice for life. It seems that the many motivational and success manuals have almost assured people that they will fail before they succeed. How absurd!

Imagine teaching your child or any child that they will fail every class in school before they will ever pass it. Yet because of the ill advice of many "life teachers", today many people live their life waiting for failure to happen so they can start having success. There are many people who have great success stories in our time today, who first had great failures. However, let's be clear and sure of one factor, that was *their* story. It doesn't have to be yours. If we live life, trying to pattern ourselves exactly like someone else's story, then we will end up living a life pieced together from all kinds of people. We'll find that we never did really live our own life.

The best about you does not have to include failure. If you have failed, you have the ability to succeed in spite of it; however, you don't have to fail to succeed. We see in the Bible for many of the Old and New Testament characters failure was not a protocol for success. Abraham did not fail to walk in the territories that God had planned for his family line. However, his father did and never inherited anything for his family. As a matter of fact, when you hear of his family line you always hear it started with Abraham, Isaac and Jacob instead of Terrah, Abraham, Isaac and Jacob.

So what happens if you do fail? You now have information of what doesn't work. So don't delay; continue to successfully complete what it is that you were asked by God to do. Seek counselors that will give you sound advice. This is a Biblical principle from

> *Proverbs 15:22 which says, "Without counsel purposes are disappointed: but in the multitude of counselors they are established."*

A qualification of counselors is further clarified in Psalm 1.

> *Psalm 1 Blessed (Happy, fortunate, prosperous, and enviable) is the man who walks and lives not in the counsel of the ungodly [following their advice, their plans and purposes], nor stands [submissive and inactive] in the path where sinners walk, nor sits down [to relax and rest] where the scornful [and the mockers] gather.*

God expects us to utilize the whole body of Christ to do what He is instructing us to do. If you read the book of Acts you see how the church continually prayed for each other, hosted each other and offered hospitality when persecution and weariness set in. While the church got together to pray for Peter, he was miraculously released from prison by an angel. In Acts 12 it was the prayer of the people of God that interceded for Peter to cause an angel to aid in his release from prison.

The key to living a successful life is to follow the instruction of the Holy Spirit, who was given to us as a guide, a teacher and a counselor (see John 14:26 and Romans 18:14). If we follow every other voice, but the voice of God, we will end up in failure. It might not happen right away; however, it will happen.

If we follow the voice of the Holy Spirit we will be led into all truth according to John 16:13.

> John 16:13 ¹³But when He, the Spirit of Truth (the Truth-giving Spirit) comes, He will guide you into all the Truth (the whole, full Truth). For He will not speak His own message [on His own authority]; but He will tell whatever He hears [from the Father; He will give the message that has been given to Him], and He will announce and declare to you the things that are to come [that will happen in the future].

We will be led into a place that we are expected to go. We are all here on the earth to fulfill a specific purpose and plan from God. The Holy Spirit is the only one that knows that plan completely. Therefore, the wise thing to do would be to listen to Him and do what He says. We develop our ability to know the voice of the Holy Spirit by spending time with God. Prayer and praise gives you experience in talking to and hearing God for yourself.

The story of Joshua in the book of Joshua is a perfect example of what happens when you follow God's instructions and don't depart from it. You will see in Joshua 1:8, God says to Joshua,

> "This Book of the Law shall not depart out of your mouth, but you shall meditate on it day and night that you may observe and do according to all that is written in it. For then you shall make your way prosperous, and then you shall deal wisely and have good success."

God was clear to Joshua that there is a way that he can walk to cause him to have a prosperous and successful journey. Since God is not a respecter of persons,

> Acts 10:34 [34]And Peter opened his mouth and said: Most certainly and thoroughly I now perceive and understand that God shows no partiality and is no respecter of persons,

we can follow the process of listening to His instructions and get the results of success.

> John 10:8 8All others who came [as such] before Me are thieves and robbers, but the [true] sheep did not listen to and obey them.

One way that we can guarantee failure, is to listen to other voices, whether it be your own, your family, friends, or co-workers that tells you the opposite of what God has instructed you to do. If that is the case, then you are being robbed. Any other voice that we follow that is not the Voice of God is a robber. John 10:8 shows this to us.

We see examples of this with King Saul. In the Old Testament, I Samuel 15, we see the story of Saul listening to his own voice to decide what success was. The Lord wanted him to kill ALL of the Amalekites and to take NONE of their spoil. That was the measure of success from God's perspective. However, in 1 Samuel 15:19-24 we see the discourse of what Saul perceived to be the "right" thing to do and what Samuel explained was supposed to really happen.

> *1 Samuel 15:19-24[19]Why then did you not obey the voice of the Lord, but swooped down upon the plunder and did evil in the Lord's sight? [20]Saul said to Samuel, Yes, I have obeyed the voice of the Lord and have gone the way which the Lord sent me, and have brought Agag king*

of Amalek and have utterly destroyed the Ama-
lekites.

In this case, we see that although Saul won the battle and overtook the enemy, including capturing King Agag, and getting all their best stuff, it was not a successful endeavor based on God's instruction. In another story in Joshua 6, we see the story of the walls of Jericho falling down. Joshua was given specific instructions of how to fight; when to strike and what to do once he entered this walled city. Joshua was not just responsible to do this himself, but he had to properly communicate to the people going with him what was the acceptable procedure for the success of this mission. It seems as though Joshua was very successful. As in verse 27, we see God's response to Joshua's mission,

> *Joshua 6:27 "So the Lord was with Joshua, and his fame was in all the land."*

Joshua was successful not because he decided to follow his plan, but he decided to follow God's instructions.

Are you ready to move forward and succeed? Then let's go!

Purpose Break

1. What is the last instruction you can remember God asking you to follow?_____

   _____

   _____

   _____

   _____

   _____

   What was your response?_____

   _____

   _____

   _____

2. Was it the results God expected? Did you think it was successful?_____

   _____

   _____

3. If you've never experienced the joy of following God's instructions, what do you think is the obstacle? *Do you feel like you don't know how to hear from God? Are you not sure if it's God or someone else or have you just thought that God couldn't possibly mean you?*_____

_____

_____

_____

_____

_____

_____

Take some time to pray in the next two days asking God to clearly speak to you through His Word and the Holy Spirit, to share with you where you've missed His instructions and where you've followed them. Take time as you are praying to write down what you sense He is saying to you. Don't worry about editing, but just document, so that you can later find scripture and seek counsel on how to follow God's instructions. Here are some scriptures to read and pray as you do this exercise: *(Note: we pray to the Father in the name of Jesus, please use your own words. I have just given you suggestions to pray below)*

> *John 10:27 - I am God's sheep and I know and hear His voice, another voice I will not follow.*
>
> *Romans 8:14 - I am led by the Spirit of God.*
>
> *I Corinthians 2:16 - I have the mind of Christ.*

Luke 22:42 - Not my will be done, but your will be done in my life. I willingly lay down my own will for my life and pickup Your will for me.

Choose other scriptures that help you in the area of hearing and obeying God's voice.

Evaluate

It is important to realize that your successful life is dependent on your successful understanding of God's instructions to you. It is worth investing time and resources in learning about God's Word (The Bible) and hearing God's voice (the Holy Spirit). These two components are so vital to helping you live a successful life. Of course, the ultimate success of your life will only come in what you actually do, not just what you heard you're supposed to do. It is a guarantee that we will succeed if we follow God's instructions. Simply put, His evaluation of our work is the deciding factor of whether or not we were successful.

A good example to consider would be in 2 Samuel 7 when King David wanted to build a house for God. But God asked him to let his son, Solomon, build it instead. If David in his zeal had disobeyed that instruction he would have failed. Instead, he made provisions for building God's house by putting wealth away so his son, Solomon, could build the temple as God said to David.

Based on the example above of David and Solomon, what has God asked you to start and give someone else to finish. To you it might seem like an unfinished project, however, to God YOUR part is finished. That's how God gets the glory for what we do, when we share the victory with others and not just boast in our own works. Your success story should always include other people.

Take some time to reflect on how this chapter has changed the way you think of success and failure.

_____

_____

_____

_____

_____

_____

_____

Decision

Make the decision to always go the way of God and not the way of your logical or natural thinking. Your life depends on your obedience to the voice of God. Listen, obey and succeed today.

Make these decisions today

1. Make a list of the previous voices that instructed you away from God's direction and
   write a big CANCELLED next to it. _____

   _____

   _____

   _____

   _____

   _____

2. Make a list of scriptures that will allow you to
   be sensitive to the voice of God. Review these
   often and especially use them when you pray
   about your life and future._____

   _____

   _____

   _____

   _____

   _____

   _____

   _____

3. Make a list of counselors God had directed you
   to in the past that have provided time-tested
   successful counsel. If you've never had anyone
   like that before, start asking God who would

qualify. Remember, even though they are giving you counsel on how to do something it is still your responsibility to obey and follow God's voice. _____

_____

_____

_____

_____

_____

_____

_____

_____

Your Future

How do you see your life success stories increasing as a result of this exercise?

Chapter Four
It's in Your Mouth!

*"The ability of your mouth muscle to produce faith or fear, is where the power to move mountains in your life exists. The power muscle you develop the most is the one that will work for your life"- **Fiona Pyszka***

*23Truly I tell you, whoever says to this mountain, Be lifted up and thrown into the sea! and does not doubt at all in his heart but believes that what he says will take place, it will be done for him. - **Mark 11:23 (AMP)***

Have you ever seen the popular game show that asks people to do something in one minute to win money? I remember seeing one of the challenges; the contestant had to take a "fish hook" type contraption in their mouth and hook pieces of metal, stacking them on each other. They had one minute to complete the task, the catch was that they had to do this without their hands assisting the process. Imagine how hard that would be! We're so used to doing things using our hands, that when a challenge involving money and a time limit comes in, we suddenly have to rethink how we move things. Although we are seeing this person do this process for the first time,

I'm sure that the contestant had practiced several times at home before actually attempting to win the money. Her practice paid off as she won the challenge within the time limit. Her practice at home was pivotal to her success on national TV with millions viewing waiting to see what would happen. Before she appeared in public she practiced in private.

The same could be said for our life. Our public life is a result of what we've been doing privately. Whether failure or success it can be directly linked back to private behavior. What we do when no one is watching or hearing us, shows up when we appear publicly. Your public life might not be in front of millions of people on television. It might be your family, your co-workers, your friends or even your social groups. Either way, you will show who you are when you are publicly on display.

We see in the book of Exodus the story of Moses, a great deliver for God's people. He did many mighty works, doing what God asked him to do. He successfully freed the slaves of Egypt (God's chosen people, the Israelites) and started them on their journey to their "promised land" from God. They were enslaved to the same masters for 430 years. That's a lot of generations with a lot of habits of just doing what they're told. As slaves they never had to fight or have their own army to defend themselves, the Egyptians took care of protection. They didn't have to figure out where food came from, they knew that their "slave labor" included the benefits of food and protection.

However, now that they were free, these benefits were no longer available from their Egyptian masters, they had to rely on their new Master, God. To help them transition to this new system, the Lord used Moses to perform miracles for provision and protection for the former slaves. This showed them firsthand how God can provide for them no matter where or who was against them. Even the way they talked to their new master, had to be renewed. Their old way was to complain to their Egyptian masters and murmur among each other when their work conditions were getting worse. They seem to have taken that same system into freedom with them. You will see in Exodus 16 and Numbers 14 accounts of murmuring and how God viewed this way as the wrong way of communicating with Him and His leaders.

God expects us to use our mouths to take hold of what He promises to us, however, the words we use are vitally important to the results we get. The children of Israel were used to doing things with their hands, being slaves to do hard labor, in order to get protection and provision. When they got in the wilderness they discovered that there was nothing they could do with their hands to provide protection or provisions. The wilderness was not conducive to planting, nor did they have any way of defending themselves against their first enemy challenge of Pharaoh and his army. They had to trust God and let His leaders help them through it.

But there was a time when God expected them to trust Him on their own, yet they were so used to the tangible, touch and feel, environment of obtaining things, that they constructed an idol that they could see and feel. A tangible "god" made from the gold that God blessed them with when they left Egypt as we see in Exodus 32.

> *Exodus 32:3-4 3 So all the people took the gold rings from their ears and brought them to Aaron. ⁴And he received the gold at their hand and fashioned it with a graving tool and made it a molten calf; and they said, These are your*

gods, O Israel, which brought you up out of the land of Egypt!

Purpose Break

1. What are some of the things you have been doing privately that you don't want people to know publicly? _____

   _____

   _____

   _____

2. What do you do publicly, to give people the illusion that you're doing "just great" that is not true privately? _____

   _____

   _____

   _____

3. What words do you actually use to describe your integrity level of truth about you that's displayed for the world to see. _____

   _____

   _____

   _____

4. Do you live a life that you would want someone to follow and act on the "big screen" for everyone to see? _____

_____

_____

_____

_____

Evaluate

As you review this chapter, take a look at some other areas that you might be holding back from pursuing because of fear.

Decision

Decide to keep moving forward using positive, faith filled words in your own mouth. Decide to stop relying on other people to do the practice of speaking for your life.

Make these decisions today

1. Write a phrase that you practice saying about yourself that will allow you to pick yourself up and move on when you feel like stopping _____

   _____

   _____

   _____

   _____

2. Write what you will stop complaining about from this day forth? _____

   _____

_____

_____

3. Write your own "declaration of independence"
    about your life. Find scriptures on God's free-
    dom to you (see Galatians 5) _____

    _____

Chapter Five
The Compounding Effect!

Everyday gives you 24 hours, your use of this time gives you the compounding effect of living in the future or from the past – **Fiona Pyszka**

And Jesus said unto him, No man, having put his hand to the plough, and looking back, is fit for the kingdom of God.
- Luke 9:62

Have you ever heard the concept of starting with a penny and doubling it for 31 days? That means, every day you double what you had the day before. So on day two you would have 2 pennies, day three 4 day five 8 and so on. On day 31 you will end up with $10,737,418.24. Now if you had stopped your doubling on day 30 you would have ended up with $5,368,709.12. Remember this all started with a penny. It's what we do with the penny that makes the difference of what happens to the penny at the end of the month. This process is called "compound interest". A concept used in the financial world to save for retirement, loan money and other ways of earning money with your money.

How much would your life change, if we considered the same strategy for our everyday life? Consider the same strategy for fulfilling what your purpose is here on earth. The biggest excuse I hear from people all the time is, "I don't have enough time, money or knowledge to do what I'm supposed to do." Well, let's see who in the Bible or in our current society has been given more than 24 hours in a day, more than one brain to work with and more than one head to get the job done, no one. As a matter of fact, you might even find people with less arms than you, missing legs, eyes that don't see, ears that can't hear, and a mouth that doesn't speak, still doing what they were made to do. The thing to always keep in mind is this, at the end of the age God will never ask us for a list of reasons why we did not finish what He asked us to do, but instead, did we do what He asked us to do?

Matthew 25 shows us this expectation in the form of a parable. The master gave out three different amounts of money to three different people. The only request was that they be good stewards of it. After a while the master returned and was ready to make reconciliation with his servants. Two of the three yielded results, they in fact doubled what was given to them.

One however, did not do anything but buried what he was given. He not only buried it, but he had harsh words against the person who gave it to him. In Matthew 25:27-28 we see the master's response,

"Then you should have invested my money with the bankers, and at my coming I would have received what was my own with interest. 28So take the talent away from him and give it to the one who has the ten talents."

According to this servant, the master was a harsh man, he was a man who reaped where he did not sow or do any work. Of course the other two servants did not pay any attention to what the character of the master was, they followed his instructions. They took the opportunity that was given to them and followed through. The servant that had a problem was already working for the man, but he suddenly had a problem when he was asked to do something on his own, without the Master-Servant motivation.

You know the type of motivation I speak of. You only do the work while the boss is around, when there is no accountability around, you simply justify why you need a break and shouldn't be working so hard. It happens every day around the world. It even happens in our school system. Children are having a hard time obeying teachers, being respectful to those in authority and we wonder what has happened to our society.

Well, maybe we should start with our homes. We need to look at how we speak of those in authority over us in different areas of our life. How we speak about the economy, about our church about the people in it, about your children's teachers etc. Your response and comments are remembered more than you realize. Your attitude gets adopted and carried onto the next generation.

So how do we break the cycle of negative compounding interest and start the trend with a positive compounding interest? How about we start with what we have. Take inventory of your gifts, talents, abilities, opportunities and position in life. Look at how much time you give to self indulgent activities that could be trimmed a little to give to someone else. These are all areas that only we can edit and change for a good result in the future. What are you willing to invest now to see the multiplied effect in your future? God speaks in terms of multiplication. It shows up in the way He made things and in the process of how He talked about sowing and reaping.

If you plant one seed in the ground, you don't reap a tree with one fruit, you will get several fruit with many seeds in them. That, my friend, is multiplication. It is compound interest at work in God's creation. We see in Genesis where God gave the order to the trees and His creation to multiply. They have been multiplying ever since. The forest is a good example of multiplication, trees keep growing as a result of seeds falling which causes more trees to grow. The same should be with our life, the people we affect will keep giving to those around them and in essence pass on what we have planted in them.

Our behavior towards those who love us and those we love will also have a compounding effect on our life. I've had the opportunity to see several couples who have been married for over 30 years. In some cases there is a positive result and in others a negative result. You see, after so many years one spouse gets tired of having to put up with the other spouse's demands. Year after year, they have to lay aside their own dreams and visions that God has given them, to carry out the dreams and vision of their spouse. After many years of failed projects and a life going nowhere, the spouse who compromised their dream to carry out the dream of the other, gets a rude awakening. "I want a divorce." Yes, the spouse who sacrificed their whole life is asked for a divorce from the one who did all the taking. Compromise in any form is against God's structure for us to live in relationship with Him and with others.

There is nowhere in the Bible where the popular "you have to compromise" message for married couples exist. Jesus never asked His church to compromise to carry out His will. Instead, He expects us to do it out of a pure and willing heart. Well a compromise is hardly pure or willing. A compromise is mostly done from fear of losing something or someone, or not wanting to face a confrontational situation. When I research the word compromise in the King James Bible I can't find it, when I look for it in other versions, there are about 3 mentions of it. All of the mentions are indicating not to compromise. Here are the examples found in the message translation. They all say to "leave or do not compromise."

> *2 Samuel 14:9 "I'll take all responsibility for what happens," the woman of Tekoa said. "I don't want to **compromise** the king and his reputation."*

2 Corinthians 6:14-18 Don't become partners with those who reject God. How can you make a partnership out of right and wrong? That's not partnership; that's war. Is light best friends with dark? Does Christ go strolling with the Devil? Do trust and mistrust hold hands? Who would think of setting up pagan idols in God's holy Temple? But that is exactly what we are, each of us a temple in whom God lives. God himself put it this way: "I'll live in them, move into them; I'll be their God and they'll be my people. So leave the corruption and **compromise**; leave it for good," says God. "Don't link up with those who will pollute you. I want you all for myself. I'll be a Father to you; you'll be sons and daughters to me." The Word of the Master, God. **Revelation 14:2-5** And then I heard music, harp music and the harpists singing a new song before the Throne and the Four Animals and the Elders. Only the 144,000 could learn to sing the song. They were bought from earth, lived without **compromise**, virgin-fresh before God. Wherever the Lamb went, they followed. They were bought from humankind, firstfruits of the harvest for God and the Lamb. Not a false word in their mouths. A perfect offering.

50

Compromising our belief and what we were sent here to do has a profound effect on our future. It affects how we will answer God when we see Him face to face. Did we do what He asked and sent us here to do? Did we listen to someone else give us the excuses of why we did not have to or could not do it? Whose will did you fulfill, yours, God's or someone else's?

Purpose Break

Take a moment to discover what things have had a compounding effect on you today.

1. What behavior or habit have you allowed to keep you back in life? _____

   _____

2. What people or groups of people have you allowed to have a compounding effect on your life? _____

   _____

   _____

3. What areas of procrastination have you allowed to compound unfinished projects in your life? _____

   _____

_____

_____

Evaluate

Take inventory of your relationships and how they affect your life. Look at the compounding effect they have had over the years or months that you have been equated.

Decision

Nothing can happen in your life unless you make a decision to accept or reject it. So list today the things that you are deciding to accept and the things you are deciding to reject. Move forward with this new arsenal of information.

Make this decision today

1. What is your plan of action to correct these un-healthy relationships and habits? _____

_____

_____

_____

Chapter Six
Who are you?

If you don't know who you are, you will never release the potential of who you are. – **Fiona Pyszka**
[16]*Your eyes saw my unformed substance, and in Your book all the days [of my life] were written before ever they took shape, when as yet there was none of them. -*
Psalm 139:16

If someone were to stop you on the street one day and asked "who are you? You might pause for a moment at their question. However, you most likely will respond with your name or even your occupation. In most cases, this answer will be sufficient and was the expectation of its initiator.

But for the purpose of this chapter, the question will require a more thorough answer and a deeper meaning to the "who are you?" A question many people have lived their whole lives unable to answer.

A few months ago, my nine year old son casually asked me on the way home one night, "Mom do you know what my purpose is?" What a profound question from such a young child. I was taken aback for a moment, then he proceeded to explain his observation. He observed that I am really good at helping people discover who they are and finding their purpose, so he thought I could help him discover his purpose so he could be sure to be on the right track.

What an incredible idea. If only we could help every child discover their purpose and thus fulfill their identity. You see, your identity and your purpose are eternally linked together. Ecclesiastes 3:11 tells us that,

> *"He has made everything beautiful in its time. He also has planted eternity in men's hearts and minds [a divinely implanted sense of a purpose working through the ages which nothing under the sun but God alone can satisfy], yet so that men cannot find out what God has done from the beginning to the end."*

Imagine being divinely created by an eternal God. Now, don't just imagine it, but believe it because it's true! The bible tells us in John 3:16 about God's gift to humanity, Jesus, because of His love for us. God sent His son to die for the sins of mankind. The sin committed in the book of Genesis separated us from God.

If you have not made Jesus the Lord of your life, then stop reading for now and go to the end of the book to make this commitment. It is the best decision you could ever make. It's a matter of life or death.

Now that you've made the best decision you can ever make, let's continue about God's plan for mankind.

His plan is eternal because He is eternal. He will never outlive His plan. He will be there forever. He wants you there with Him. That was the whole plan. But we see in Genesis 3 where this plan started to unravel.

Your Identity Includes Equality

To understand our identity we do need to go back to Genesis. So let's take a look at chapter 1.

> **Genesis 1:27** *So God created man in His own image, in the image and likeness of God He created him; male and female He created them.*

As you can see in Genesis 1:27, we were created in the image of God. Both male and female were created in His likeness. Not just the male or just the female. We see in the beginning we were created equally like God's image, both male and female.

There were no equality issues in the garden of Eden. There were no gender issues. Both male and female were created in the image of God. To get your true identity you have to go back to God's image of you and His intended purpose for creating mankind.

Your Identity Includes the Blessing to Multiply

Let's read further in Chapter 1,

> *Genesis 1:28 And God blessed them and said to them, Be fruitful, multiply, and fill the earth, and subdue it [using all its vast resources in the service of God and man]; and have dominion over the fish of the sea, the birds of the air, and over every living creature that moves upon the earth.*

We see here that God had an expectation of both the male and female because He blessed them both. He expected them to be fruitful and multiply and fill the earth. They were to use its resources to give service to God and to man. Notice the order there, first God then man. Dominion was to be expressed to the animals, birds, fish and other creatures that God created. Dominion was never expected to be administered from one human to another.

Are you starting to get a picture of what your foundational identity looks like? Are you starting to develop an inward image of eternal life instead of seething hopelessness? You should. You were created in the image of the Creator of the universe. He created the trees that produce, the earth that brings forth fruit in its season. He created the birds of the air and fish of the sea. All of which provide food for us. How can such an incredible being create us in His likeness and leave out the creative part.

Your Identity Includes Creativity

What you lack you can create. God made us to create new, to create change, to create solutions. He showed us how to do it too. In Genesis 1, God came on the scene to void, formless, darkness. What did He do first? He created. God created first. He made something out of nothing. What was, and still is, the key ingredient to God's creativity? The answer is found in Genesis 1:3,

> *Genesis 1:3 And God said, Let there be light; and there was light.*

Do you see the answer? It is found in the word "said". Yes, what we say will determine what we create. What we create will hinder or help our identity. The bible tells us this about the words of our mouth.

Proverbs 6:2 "You are snared with the words of your lips, you are caught by the speech of your mouth."

To be snared is to be caught. Imagine being caught in a trap by your own words. Words that tie up your future and tie down your potential. Words that break your heart and bind your soul. These are words that are produced everyday by people created to create.

Imagine what kind of a clothing line a fashion designer will produce if they constantly cut their creation with their scissors. Every time they did not like what someone said about their design, or they did not like the stitch they just made, they take their scissors and cut parts of the design to pieces. What will be the end result, most likely, unrecognizable.

It's the same way with people. A person can use their words in such a harsh way about their own life that they become unrecognizable. But you may say, I don't say bad things about myself, my spouse does, or my boss does, or my parents do. By accepting these words it's like we are saying them.

God gave us the power of attorney for our own life. Jesus demonstrated this when He said about His life and assignment,

> John 10:17-19 [17]For this [reason] the Father loves Me, because I lay down My [own] life--to take it back again. [18]No one takes it away from Me. On the contrary, I lay it down voluntarily. [I put it from Myself.] I am authorized and have power to lay it down (to resign it) and I am authorized and have power to take it back again. These are the instructions (orders) which I have received [as My charge] from My Father.

Our life is our responsibility. It is our duty to our heavenly Father to take good care of it. Whether you are struggling with eating habits that harm your life, spouses that abuse you verbally or physically, bosses, or bullies, none of them have the authority from God to have the last word in your life, you do!

In the chapters ahead we will define and refine concepts of how to get out from under identity theft and find you again. Or for some of you, you will find answers to your more in-depth question of "how do I know if who I think I am, is who I am suppose to be?"

Purpose Break

1. Do you see how your identity originates with God's view of you? _____

2. What do you think God thinks about you? _____

    _____

    _____

    _____

3. Have you made the decision to have eternal life with Christ? _____

    _____

4. Do you compare yourself with others? _____

    _____

5. If so, in what way do you compare yourself? ___

    _____

    _____

6. What do these comparisons do for you? _____

    _____

    _____

    _____

7. Based on your answer to 6, should you continue these comparisons? _____

8. God created you to be creative, what is the creative thing that God created you to do? ____

    _____

9. What are some of the creative things that you have done so far in your life? _____

_____

_____

_____

Evaluate

Now let's practically identify some things about you. Take the time to think about and write answers as you can think of them. Don't over analyze the answers, these questions should be answered with ease, as that best describes what your real belief is.

1. Who do you think you are? If I stopped you on the street with that question, what would the answer be? _____

_____

_____

_____

_____

2. Do you currently express who you are fully, or are you in "witness" protection with your identity? _____ If yes, who are you hiding your identity from? _____

_____

Why _____

_____

_____

3. Do you want to express your true identity to the world? _____

Chapter Seven
Where Does Identity Come From?

Your identity should not change because of your circums-tances. **Fiona Pyszka**

"Before I formed you in the womb I knew you, before you were born I set you apart; I appointed you as a prophet to the nations." **Jeremiah 1:5**

The big trend today is for people to go and find themselves. The expectation is that if only one could find themselves then they would be happy. I agree, being who you were meant to be will give you a much healthier, happier, fulfilling life. However, going somewhere to find who you are is a hopeless endeavor. For when you arrive at that somewhere you will still be you. You were never missing, lost or of no value. You only needed to find out from God, your creator, what He sent you here to do.

Who you are comes built into your spirit. It is forever engraved in your DNA. It's who we've become that makes it impossible to live with or fulfill our dreams. If we find that who we've become is less than what we've dreamed of, we then become withdrawn, frustrated or depressed.

Jesus was confident as a human when He walked the earth. He continually told people who He was and why He was here. He never tried to hide anything. He was eager to fulfill His responsibility.

Our identity is our responsibility to fulfill for the glory of God. We were created in God's image to do what He asked us to do. We are to use His image in us to multiply, subdue, replenish and create. Why do I say this? Remember in a previous chapter we discussed how in Genesis God blessed mankind through Adam and Eve to be fruitful and multiply and create and do all the things we stated? So what happened next? Adam and Eve did multiply and they were fruitful, however, mankind became vile before God and a big event in history happened, the flood! It wiped out everything that had multiplied except for Noah and his family, who were protected in the ark. After the flood, let's see what God said to Noah. Look at Genesis chapter 9,

> Genesis 9 [1]AND GOD pronounced a blessing upon Noah and his sons and said to them, Be fruitful and multiply and fill the earth. [2]And the

64

fear of you and the dread and terror of you shall be upon every beast of the land, every bird of the air, all that creeps upon the ground, and upon all the fish of the sea; they are delivered into your hand. ³Every moving thing that lives shall be food for you; and as I gave you the green vegetables and plants, I give you everything.

Sounds similar to what was said in Genesis 1 to Adam and Eve right? You see God is very clear on His intentions for placing us here. His intention was to have us do on earth what is done in heaven. Sounds familiar? Let's look at another passage of scripture:

Matthew 6:9-10 ⁹Pray, therefore, like this: Our Father Who is in heaven, hallowed (kept holy) be Your name. ¹⁰Your kingdom come, Your will be done on earth as it is in heaven.

The disciples requested that Jesus teach them how to pray. His response is what we see in Matthew 6. In verse 10 we see that he instructs them to pray that God's will be done on earth as it is in heaven. Who will God use on earth to fulfill His will? Of course it will be you and I. We are the ones sent to earth to fulfill God's will.

Do you see the importance of securing who you are so that you can fulfill what you are suppose to be for God.

Identity Rescue

When man sinned as noted in Genesis 3, he gave over his powerful position, of owner and they became slaves, of God's enemy, Satan. Now, man had to "survive" instead of just live. Man's eternal identity was compromised to now include a ticking time bomb, physical death. At the moment of sin, man was immediately cut off from his spirit man being connected to God. God had to reverse this mistake and sin of man so that His original intention "eternal life" could still happen. That's why Jesus came.

Sin took man's identity from ownership to slavery in a moment. Instead of living by his spirit, man now had to do things just so his flesh could stay alive longer. Sound familiar? What are people doing today to keep their flesh alive longer? What do they do just to be able to live in their own skin? Man needed an identity rescue.

A rescue from slave to free lost to found. A picture of this is told in the Exodus story of the children of

Israel. We see in Exodus 12 the breakthrough of God rescuing His people from the hands of slavery.

> *Exodus 12:30-32* [30]*Pharaoh rose up in the night, he, all his servants, and all the Egyptians; and there was a great cry in Egypt, for there was not a house where there was not one dead.* [31]*He called for Moses and Aaron by night, and said, Rise up, get out from among my people, both you and the Israelites; and go, serve the Lord, as you said.* [32]*Also take your flocks and your herds, as you have said, and be gone! And [ask your God to] bless me also.*

God rescued His people at night. He rescued them in a moment. Take some time and read the rest of the story in Exodus 12 you'll see how God's people were rescued in a hurry. They were in such a hurry that their bread was not able to rise. Thus they had unleavened bread.

Imagine the scene. The moment had come for them to be rescued. Now their years, 430 to be exact, of slavery was about to be over. That means there were generations of slavery represented in the people. Imagine generations of people who didn't know anything else but slavery. Not one free day had ever existed in their life. They don't know what it feels like to do something without asking permission. They never had the opportunity to envision their own dreams being fulfilled. The only dream they all had was to be rescued from being a slave. What that feels like or what responsibility that entailed, they had no concept of. You see, they all had the same problem, they were slaves. None of them had a bigger vision other than to get out from under the Egyptians.

They wanted to be rescued from slavery into something they had not experienced. They wanted to be anywhere but there. For generations there was no vision of a Jew being free. All the children born during that time only knew a household that worked as a slave for its masters, the Egyptians. The Egyptians for generations never saw a free Jew either. Both groups played their parts in this cascading ride through history.

But tonight, this night, the story changes for everyone. The Jews are being set free. Their cries have been heard. The command was given for the Jews to rise up and leave. But they didn't have to leave empty handed. They were asked to take the jewelry of their "masters" with them. Further in Exodus 12 we see this.

> *Exodus 12:35-36*[35]*The Israelites did according to the word of Moses; and they [urgently] asked of the Egyptians jewels of silver and of gold, and clothing.* [36]*The Lord gave the people favor in the sight of the Egyptians, so that they gave them what they asked. And they stripped the Egyptians [of those things].*

You have to get a picture of this scene of delivery. It was in the middle of the night, the Egyptians are experiencing something they never experienced before, favor towards their slaves. The Jews are experiencing what they've never experienced before, favor from their masters. It was also a scene of high emotions and activity. It was a suddenly!

A suddenly moment when God said, "now is the time to leave. My deliverance has arrived." The moment occurred when every Egyptian household was mourning the loss of their first born of everything. That means their children and their livestock. Any person or animal that was the first born of Egypt encountered the death angel that night.

Exodus 12:29-30 [29]*At midnight the Lord slew every firstborn in the land of Egypt, from the firstborn of Pharaoh who sat on his throne to the firstborn of the prisoner in the dungeon, and all the firstborn of the livestock.* [30]*Pharaoh rose up in the night, he, all his servants, and all the Egyptians; and there was a great cry in Egypt, for there was not a house where there was not one dead.*

What a scene. Every house in the country had a dead person being mourned. A decrease in assets as their livestock lost its firstborn as well. It was during this time that the Lord asked the Jews to leave their situation of slavery. This was the only identity they knew. The only "job" they ever had. This was the generational occupation, "slavery". They cried out to God for a change, when change came it came quickly.

What is your identity situation? Are you crying out for an identity rescue? The answer lies in following the voice of God for you to rise up when He tells you to. Sometimes we miss our moment of delivery. We miss our moment of being set free because of the unusual way it may happen, or the suddenly of how instruction comes.

70

God gave the instruction to Moses to give to the children of Israel (the Jews) but they could have all said "no, we want to be free this way." Or "I have worked for this family for so long, I can't just up and leave them." Or "I don't know what else I am going to do, so I have to keep doing this until I see what the new thing will turn out to be." All of these excuses hold you back into a false identity.

False Identity

A false identity can become so real that a person forgets where they came from or what they were created to be. It can be used to escape undetected or to blend in where you are. Examine yourself today to see if you are operating under a false identity. Here are some questions that will help:

1. Do you find yourself being one way at home and a different way at work or church or in your social interactions?
2. When you're around "certain groups of people or a person" do you change to show a different side of you?

3. Do you hold back being "yourself" when inte-
    racting with certain people or in certain situa-
    tions?

If you find that you are participating in any of the
above situations, you might be hiding your identity to
"keep the peace" or just survive.

Over the years I've heard stories of and spoken to
people who have been abused. Whether it was sex-
ually, physically or emotionally, the person would explain that they coped with it by either being who the
other person wanted them to be, by holding part of
themselves back, or pretending to be someone different all together that they create in their mind. Hence,
in my opinion, the reality of many people dealing with
multiple personality syndromes and split personality
disorders.

I am not a psychologist and so by no means do I
speak of these abnormalities with expertise, I only
speak of them from my own experience of interaction
with these hurting people. I've seen men and women
crying at the thought that they were put on earth with
a purpose from God. The idea that they can fulfill a
vision and have a dream for their life is a foreign con-

cept, one that they secretly hoped for but publicly denied. What is your story? Have you hidden a part of you to cover up your true identity? Are you moving along life's corridors under the pretense of being someone else? Someone man created and not God.

To discover whether or not you are operating in a "false identity" mode, consider the following questions.

Purpose Break

1. What's the last instruction you feel God asked you to fulfill? _____

2. What did you do with that instruction? _____

   _____

3. Did you start it and stopped in the middle of completion because of what man did or said? _

   _____

4. Did you even bother to do it at all? _____

5. Who holds the keys to unlocking your identity? Is it you, or someone else?_____

These questions are vital to be answered in order to wake us up to the reality of who we have been pretending to be. The real you, as created by God, will

NEVER want to disobey God. The only way you would disobey would be with outside influence. We see this phenomenon happened in Genesis 3 when Eve was deceived by God's enemy, Satan.

Make no mistake about it, Satan will always interfere with God's children in order to sidetrack, distract, or re-label them for his benefit. If you're not operating in life for God's benefit, then you are either operating for your personal gain or being controlled by Satan for his glory. Don't be one of his victims. Become victorious through Jesus. Never take God's "go" and replace it with someone else's "no".

Jesus is the way and became the door for us to get connected back to God. Let's go through Him to find our true identity and get reconnected again for good.

Who you are in Christ

Your true identity can only be found in who you have become in Christ. You are a new creation in Christ Jesus, old things have passed away, all things have become new (2 Corinthians 5:17). The passing away of the old you might have happened years ago. Maybe you are reading this saying that you became a new creation in Christ years ago, but you are still struggling with who you are. You're not alone. Later on we will look further into what to do if you feel you have lost who you are or who you use to be.

In the meantime, examine these scriptures that tell us who we are in Christ to determine if you have been missing out on what God has made available for you.

> *Romans 8:2 For the law of the Spirit of life [which is]* **in Christ** *Jesus [the law of our new being] has freed me from the law of sin and of death.*

Looking at this verse, here are some questions to ask yourself: What law do you live by? Are you still living under the curse of sin and death? Even though you are born again, have you switched living arrangements? Do you submit to God's Spirit of life? It's easy to figure out which law you are living by. Do you long to be able to do God's will, but find yourself saying things like "if only I was more educated, spiritual, happier " (you fill in the blank). Is your ability to fulfill God's inquiries being hampered by a perceived obstacle in your path? Like having more money or being in a different family or even growing up in a different country.

The law of sin and death is a process of "hard labor", negative environment and outward appearances. The law of sin and death is about production without instruction, action without satisfaction. The fruit of the law of sin and death is always loss. It might not be immediate, but it does show up as the end result.

You might have now recognized loss of who you are, or loss of who you use to be. This loss is an indication that you have been functioning without the power of Christ's sacrifice on the cross. He acted on your behalf for you to live through Him. What does it mean to live through Christ? It means protection, surrender and direction.

> *Colossians 2:3-4 3In Him all the treasures of [divine] wisdom (comprehensive insight into the ways and purposes of God) and [all the riches of spiritual] knowledge and enlightenment are stored up and lie hidden. ⁴I say this in order that no one may mislead and delude you by plausible and persuasive and attractive arguments and beguiling speech.*

Our identity lies hidden in Christ. He has given us the keys to unlock who God created us to be, the keys of life through His work on the cross. Jesus came to give you life and life more abundantly, see John 10:10. It was for freedom that Christ has set you free, see Galatians 5:1.

> *Galatians 5 [1]IN [this] freedom Christ has made us free [and completely liberated us]; stand fast then, and do not be hampered and held ensnared and submit again to a yoke of slavery [which you have once put off].*

These truths become the arsenal by which you overcome the enemy and his cohorts that have launched an attack on your identity. Jesus set you free so that you can live freely. Therefore, live freely by being who you know you should be, the person that has been longing to show others the true you.

God has not given authority to any position or person on earth that would hinder our purpose for Him. No one was given dominion over man in the Garden of Eden, referring to "male" or "female". Jesus never reprimanded people for coming to Him to fulfill His Father's will. He expected them to put some things aside so that they can freely follow the Father. This is our example for following God's will in our life without compromise. Look at this exchange,

Luke 14:26 *If anyone comes to Me and does not hate his [own] father and mother [in the sense of indifference to or relative disregard for them in comparison with his attitude toward God] and [likewise] his wife and children and brothers and sisters--[yes] and even his own life also--he cannot be My disciple.*

Now in no way was Jesus saying to get a divorce, leave your parents house (if you're a minor) or totally shut yourself away from family. What He was saying though is more a statement of priority. What priority does God have in your life? Does He come after everyone else has been fulfilled with their longing for your time, energies and talents? Or is His the last opinion considered when making critical decisions in life? You make these decisions based on how your view yourself. Are you the slave of someone in your life? Are you a slave to their bad attitude, negative spewing or unfulfilled passions?

If your identity is compromised your purpose is hindered. Your future is stalled. Your dreams die. God's vision for you is greater than your thoughts could ever be of yourself. Therefore, it is wise to hook up to His dreams for you. Your identity was created to handle His dreams for you.

Evaluate

1. Understand you were created in God's image. Your identity came from Him. Write some things down that you equate with God's view of you: _____

   _____

   _____

2. Rescue your identity from the traps of the enemy. The traps he sets through people, circumstances and your mind. Who are the people traps you may need to review? _____

   _____

   _____

   _____

3. Learn who you are in Christ Jesus. List some scriptures (see Colossians and Ephesians) that you find speaks to your spirit about who you are in Christ: _____

   _____

   _____

Decision

Take some time to answer these questions about you. Answer as best you can recall. Don't leave it to do later, that can be a distraction that cost you your momentum so far.

Make these decisions today

1. Describe what you would do if no one told you that you were incapable of doing it? _____

   _____

   _____

2. What people group would you help today, if you had no obstacles? _____

   _____

   _____

   _____

3. Now, what are the obstacles you face? _____

   _____

   _____

   _____

   _____

Chapter Eight
A King in the House

People may observe, evaluate and guess at who you are, but it is God who has the final answer. Therefore, take His Word for it. - **Fiona Pyszka**

[16]*Your eyes saw my unformed substance, and in Your book all the days [of my life] were written before ever they took shape, when as yet there was none of them.* - **Psalm 139:16**

Imagine having a king in your house and not knowing it, a leader of a nation, the owner of a crown, the office of royalty, all living in your house. How would you treat that person differently if you knew they were a king? What accommodations would you make to see to it that they had what they needed to grow and mature?

David who defeated Goliath was such a person. He was a king living in a house full of people who never thought of him as more than a "boy" who took care of a few sheep. His brother mocked him. If you read the story of his anointing to be king, you will find that he was not even invited to the dinner (1 Samuel 16:11).

1 Samuel 17:28 [28]Now Eliab his eldest brother heard what he said to the men; and Eliab's anger was kindled against David and he said, Why did you come here? With whom have you left those few sheep in the wilderness? I know your presumption and evilness of heart; for you came down that you might see the battle.

Guess what? You do have a king living in your house. Whether male or female you are a king and priest unto the Lord. To help you handle this truth, if you are a woman, you can consider the word king as a queen. Either way royalty is in your new DNA structure as a Christian.

1 Peter 2:9 But you are a chosen race, a royal priesthood, a dedicated nation, [God's] own purchased, special people, that you may set forth the wonderful deeds and display the virtues and perfections of Him Who called you out of darkness into His marvelous light.

Revelation 5:10 10And You have made them a kingdom (royal race) and priests to our God, and they shall reign [as kings] over the earth!

Romans 8:17 And if we are [His] children, then we are [His] heirs also: heirs of God and fellow heirs with Christ [sharing His inheritance with

Him]; only we must share His suffering if we are to share His glory.

Because of Jesus, we are now royalty in the Kingdom of God. We are heirs with Christ Jesus to the things that the Father has stored up for us. One of those things is our purpose. Our purpose was designed by God for such a time as this. We are uniquely made and intricately designed. Every fiber of your being holds your purpose.

> *Psalm 139:15-16 My frame was not hidden from You when I was being formed in secret [and] intricately and curiously wrought [as if embroidered with various colors] in the depths of the earth [a region of darkness and mystery]. ¹⁶Your eyes saw my unformed substance, and in Your book all the days [of my life] were written before ever they took shape, when as yet there was none of them.*

Have you ever found yourself loving something with "every fiber of your being" or hated something just the same? These are clues to the things that lead us to our purpose. In the next chapters of this book we will look at some questions that you can filter through to get heading in the right direction to fulfil your purpose. We will also look at how you can create a plan to get this accomplished.

God had a plan. We call it the "plan of salvation" today. His plan was Jesus. Jesus had a mission based on God's plan. Your plan will give you a mission. If you live life without a mission, you will be aimlessly wondering around life, frustrated, unfulfilled and controlled.

The enemy can easily control someone who does not know what they're supposed to do. He will give them his assignment complete with open doors. Yes, just because a door is open does not mean that it's a way that you should go. The opposite is also true, just because a door is closed does not mean that it's an indicator of a way that we should stay out of. Our direction should come only from the Holy Ghost.

> **Romans 8:14** *For all who are led by the Spirit of God are sons of God.*

If we decide to be a child of God, then we must also follow the instructions of God. Follow Him by way of His Holy Spirit not by way of fleeces, open or closed doors. These are all things that should be subject to us, not us be subject to them. I have helped many people over the years who have thought that if God wanted them to have something He would open the door. They ended up with a closed door life. Or they would walk through every open door, thinking that God wanted them to or He would have shut them. God is not a game show host. He is Almighty God. His Word is powerful and meaningful. He expects us to follow His Word. He doesn't want us to follow doors, opportunities or circumstances. He wants us to follow Him. His Holy Spirit is Him!

Purpose Break

Consider today the following questions about how you feel about yourself.

1. What "peasant" thoughts have you had about yourself lately? _____

_____

_____

_____

2. What "kingly/queenly" thoughts have you had about yourself lately? _____

_____

_____

_____

_____

3. Which thoughts would you rather see become a reality? _____

_____

_____

_____

Evaluate

As you answer the questions, consider focusing your future thoughts on what you would rather see happen from now on. Practice staying away from thoughts of the past that only produced loss or death. Your future requires the leverage and momentum of life. Don't give your future thoughts of death and defeat.

1. List some words that are positive faith filled words that can help you think better thoughts of your future. *(hint: find scriptures that speak to you life, they will contain words for you to add to your daily vocabulary)* _____

_____

_____

_____

Chapter Nine

The Purpose of You

Your purpose is yours alone. Therefore, there is never a need to compete to fulfill your destiny.

Fiona Pyszka

Many are the plans in a person's heart, but it is the LORD's purpose that prevails. **Proverbs 19:21**

In this chapter you will be discovering who you are though a series of questions. It is a process of evaluating what you have to correct. Our purpose is wrapped up in us. Discovering it is our job. These questions are designed to help you pull out things that you already know about yourself. Let's lay it all out on the table and see what God has planned for you before ever a day of your life got started.

1. What are your current positions in life (mother/father, daughter/son, husband/wife, job position etc) _____

_____

_____

2. Are you satisfied with those positions? _____

_____

3. Why or why not? _____

_____

4. What position would you like to add to the future? _

_____

5. When you die, what would you like people to say
   about you _____

_____

_____

6. Do they have enough evidence to say that about
   you now? _____

7. Why or why not? _____

_____

8. What are your plans to secure what people say
   about you at death? (for example, if you wanted to
   be known as the greatest inventor in the world,
   once you've succeeded at the first greatest inven-
   tion in the world, what are your plans to keep it
   that way – so that you keep inventing to stay being
   the greatest inventor in the world) _____

_____

_____

_____

_____

_____

9. What is the standard you live your life by? _____

_____

10. Who has the most influence about the standard of your life? (i.e., the person you look up to the most)

_____

_____

11. Why? _____

_____

12. What is the greatest thing that person (your standard) has ever accomplished? _____

_____

13. Are they still alive? _____

14. Do you have the potential to be greater than they are or were? _____

15. Why? _____

_____

16. Are you satisfied with that answer? _____

17. Do you feel or believe that your standard (person you base it on) should outlive you or the other way around? _____

_____

18. Who are your heroes – dead or alive? _____

_____

19. Why? What is the one common characteristic of them all? _____

20. Based on the information just given, do you see the need to change any part of your standard? If yes, what would you change?_____

_____

_____

_____

21. Do you have a written plan that helps you stay on track for the future? _____

22. Do you have the skill set needed to communicate and motivate people around you that could help

you accomplish your purpose for your life? _____

_____

23. Why or why not? _____

_____

24. How do you keep replenishing your information pool for your purpose to be accomplished? _____

_____

_____

25. What's the best way for you to retain vital information for your life to run smoothly? (e.g., reading, doing, seeing, feeling, speaking etc.) _____

_____

26. Paint a picture of your future with words – what would the main words of your future say about your relationship and influence with:_____

_____

a. Your Spouse _____

_____

_____

b. Your child/children _____

_____

c. Your company/employees/employers _____

_____

d. Your God _____

_____

_____

e. Your purpose for being on earth _____

_____

_____

27. With your current lifestyle and the plan you have laid out for your life, are you on track for doing exactly what you're here on the earth to do? _____

_____

28. Why or why not? _____

_____

Questions to stimulate and help you further discover your purpose in life

1. What makes you angry or sad whenever it happens? _____

2. Who do you find yourself wanting to help the most? _____

3. What's the longest job you ever kept? Why? _____

_____

4. What was the thing you loved the most to do in life, whether hobby or job, paid or unpaid? _____

_____

_____

5. What adjectives (action words) do you like the most? What words move you to do something

_____

_____

_____

6. Finish this sentence: I am the best at _____

_____

_____

_____

7. How did you learn the skills that you are the best in _____

_____

_____

_____

8. Do you enjoy doing these things? _____

_____

9. Which skill is your best skill?_____

_____

10. Which do you enjoy doing the most? _____

_____

11. Who (person or people group) do I want to affect the most on this earth? _____

_____

12. How do I want to affect them – what gifts and talents do I want to use? _____

_____

13. What will the results of my affect on their life look like? _____

_____

14. How long does it take me to help someone? _____

_____

15. What prevents me from wanting to help the people I want to help the most? _____

Chapter Ten
The Plan

God's plan for you is eternal. He does not have to change it to accommodate our circumstances – **Fiona Pyszka**
10Declaring the end and the result from the beginning, and from ancient times the things that are not yet done, saying, My counsel shall stand, and I will do all My pleasure and purpose, - **Isaiah 46:10**

For any purpose to be successful, we must commit to it. This is the moment of commitment. You have a decision to make. Will you commit to your future, or continue to procrastinate with a bag full of excuse of who and why?

By now, if you have taken time to answer the questions in the previous chapters, you should be well on your way to believing that you are more than you thought you were. Even if you thought you were great and can do anything. You should still have seen more great things that God created in you and for you.

Following are some questions that will help you develop a plan to fulfill the purpose you have discovered that God has put in you. There is no one on earth that was born without a purpose. Therefore, a plan is necessary for everyone. God had a plan, we see his mission statement in John 3:16. We see the unfolding of His plan throughout the ages. God wrote His plan down so that we will run with it.

> **Habakkuk 2:2** *And **the** Lord answered me and said, **Write the vision** and engrave it so plainly upon tablets that everyone who passes may [be able to] read [it easily and quickly] as he hastens by.*

God did for us exactly what His instruction says in Habakkuk 2:2. He has given us 66 books containing His plans. He shows us where we came from, what we are to do while we're here, and what happens when we leave here.

Like God's plan, our plan can be accepted or rejected by those around us. It doesn't mean that we should continue or stop based on people's response. We should continue with God's plan if He gave it to us. We should stop it when He tells us to stop. In other words, just like God did not remove salvation from His offerings because of man's rejection, even so we should not remove the action of our purpose from our life because of our past or any future rejections.

96

Make your decision now, that you will ask God for the core of the plan He has already written for your life (see Psalm 139:16). Let's look at some questions that will help you get to that goal.

The following is a personalized look at how to get your purpose in life fulfilled. Remember this is a life-time achievement, it's not a once and done thing. It starts with something that's always bigger than you, but it continues with something that can grow into the level and expertise that you never dreamed of. I can guarantee you that your biggest dreams are not big enough yet for what you could possibly accomplish in your lifetime.

How much time are you willing to give per week towards fulfilling your purpose in life _____

1. What do I need to do in the next 3 months to steer me in the direction of my purpose, goals and accomplishments?

    a.

    b.

    c.

    d.

    e.

    f.

2. What are the results of the past 3 months?

    a.

    b.

    c.

    d.

    e.

    f.

3. What happens after three months?

    a.

    b.

    c.

    d.

    e.

    f.

4. Did I fulfill all of my goals – what were the obstacles?

    a. Do I have control over the obstacles?

    b. Can I avoid them in the future?

    c. Do I have a habit that needs managed to help me accomplish my goals for the future?

5. What have I realized about myself?

6. Can I take this model into my future to apply to every area of my life?

7. What are the key relationships that can help me build my future goals and dreams?

The new information that you have just gathered about yourself will aid you in creating a written plan for your future. Don't worry about not knowing what will happen in the future, just focus on what areas of your life you would like to get in order. Start with those areas.

A written plan can consist of the following information. Since this is your plan you can set it up whatever way you desire. Put no limits on it, but here is a guideline you can use to get you started.

The Plan

Your plan should include a vision statement.

1. A vision statement is a sentence or two that best describes what you would like to do

99

with your life. Don't' worry about what you don't know.

Write about what your heart's desire is to do. For example:"My vision is to see the epidemic of "sex trafficking" be eliminated from the world". Making a statement like that denotes a very large vision. However, God had a vision to have the "whole world" not perish but have everlasting life (John 3:16). Not all men will receive salvation. Nevertheless, a plan has been put in place that gives men the chance to receive salvation.

Similarly, your vision might be vast (don't try to make it small) and you might not think that it's possible for just you to do it. The great news is that whatever God asked us to do, will need to include people to help us. But like He stated in Habakkuk 2:2, we have to write it and make it plain so that people could run with it.

2. Make a list of what you would need to do to fulfill this vision. *List what you know now. Things can be added later. Especially as you meet people.*

3. Don't worry about the format. The format should be that it is clear for people who

need to review it to help you. So a list format is good, paragraph format is good.

4. Add appropriate scriptures to accommodate your plan and what you see the Lord telling you.

Your plan can be as long or short as it needs to be. Don't be concerned about those details. The main thing is that you write something down. Then you follow through and do something with it. If you see your plans are beyond what you can do, then you pray and ask God to get you the help you need. You ask God to train you in the areas you need training. When you ask, you must wait for an answer and follow whatever instructions you receive.

This is an important plan of fulfilling your God given purpose. Do not skip this part. Of all the things you could do with this book, the last two chapters are the most important follow through exercises.

I pray that you have all of God's purposes for you fulfilled in your lifetime. May your dreams continue to come true. May all the resources and help you need be lavished on you. May God's Will be done in your life continually.

The Ultimate Plan

Salvation

The best plan that you can follow in your life is the plan to follow Jesus. To make Him your Lord and Savior. Man is born into sin and need a savior. Jesus came to take our sins for us. He became our Savior. If you have never made Jesus the Lord of your life or accepted Him as your Savior, then this is your moment. Follow the plan that yields eternal life. Say this prayer with me:

Heavenly Father, in the Name of Jesus, I present myself to You. I pray and ask Jesus to be Lord over my life. I confess that I am a sinner, I need salvation. I receive Jesus as my salvation. I believe it in my heart, so I say it with my mouth: This moment, I make Him the Lord over my life. Jesus, come into my heart. I believe this moment that I am saved, I say it now: "I am reborn. I am a Christian. I am a child of Almighty God." Amen.

Scriptures

John 3:16 For God so greatly loved *and* dearly prized the world that He [even] gave up His only begotten (unique) Son, so that whoever believes in (trusts in, clings to, relies on) Him shall not perish (come to destruction, be lost) but have eternal (everlasting) life.

Contact us:

If you took this step today to receive Jesus as your Savior, we want to hear about it. Contact us at:

fionap@fionainc.com

717-917-8101

For more information about Fiona Inc, visit us at our website, www.fionainc.com. While there, check out our free resources available to you. You may also purchase teachings and other valuable information.

Fiona also meets one-on-one with clients to help them further develop and pursue their purpose. If you would like to setup your own personalized session, email us for details.

If the information in this book has changed your life, we want to hear about it. So contact us today!

Visit us on facebook to share your experience:

http://www.facebook.com/discoverfionainc